LIVING THE DREAM IN
Los Angeles

LIVING THE DREAM IN
Los Angeles

101 Practical Points You Should Know When Moving From The UK

CHARLOTTE HARRIS

First published 2019

ISBN (paperback): 978-1-09790-621-5
ISBN (e-book): not applicable

LivingTheDreamBooks.com

Cover design by Madeeha Shaikh (DezignManiac)

A catalogue record for this book is available from the British Library.

To every person, young or old,
who dreams of adventures, and then
takes a brave step towards them.

Contents

LIVING THE DREAM IN
Los Angeles

INTRODUCTION

You've made the decision and you're on your way to the land of glitz, glamour, palm trees, beach yoga, green juices, and tiny dogs; Los Angeles. Your new home for the next chapter of your life. How do you feel? Nervous or not, it's an exhilarating place to move to.

Moving abroad brings many new challenges, raising questions we had never thought to ask. It's wondering 'where's the nearest supermarket?' followed quickly by thinking 'what are the supermarkets even called?'. It's asking how much something is, then deliberating over how much you're expected to tip. It's standing in a homeware store and questioning why the bedding section doesn't contain duvet covers. Or searching for eggs in a supermarket and then wondering why they need to be kept in the fridge.

Maybe you're the type of person who takes everything in their stride, immersing yourself into new places by observing those around you. Or perhaps you prefer to rely on the experiences of others, researching topics online or talking to friends who have moved abroad. Whichever your preference, this book arms you with the answers to those unknown questions turning you from tourist to local before you can say Taco Tuesday.

So, read on to find out what you must do when parking on hills, how to sound like a local when giving directions, and why you can fill up both your car and your shopping bags hands-free - allowing you to grab your sunglasses and a vegan, alkaline, crystal-infused, chlorophyll water (yes, this exists) - and start exploring Los Angeles sooner. After all, that's when you start living the dream!

ARRIVING

USA ENTRY REQUIREMENTS

1. To gain entry to the United States you need a valid passport, with an expiry date any point beyond the period of your intended visit. Your purpose of travel and length of stay will dictate if you need a Visa.

- Personal trips up to 90 days:
  - → Many British citizens qualify for the Visa Waiver Program and can travel on an Electronic System for Travel Authorisation (ESTA).
  - → Apply for an ESTA online and at least 72 hours in advance of your flight.
  - → An ESTA costs $14, anywhere charging you more is a scam site.
  - → Screenshot the confirmation page showing your application reference number, as you will not receive a copy over email.
  - → ESTAs are valid for 2 years, unless you update your passport.
  - → US Customs also require you to purchase a return flight back to the UK before you arrive in the US.

- Personal trips more than 90 days:
  You need to apply for a Visa and attend an interview at the US Embassy in London. Check the US Embassy website to find the correct Visa.

- Business trips:
  Talk to your employer to understand which Visa you need and if you are required to attend an interview at the US Embassy.

FLYING & JET LAG

2. When flying to LA, aim to depart on an early morning flight as there's a smaller chance that your flight will be delayed.

3. Beat the queues at LAX airport by applying to the Global Entry program, which enables fast-track customs clearance for pre-approved travellers landing in the US. The application involves a rigorous background check and in-person interview before enrolment.

4. Drink plenty of water on the flight to help you avoid jet lag. Take an empty bottle with you through airport security and fill it up before you board. Aim to drink at least 2 litres of water during the 10-11 hour flight.

5. Resist both napping and going to bed early on the day you arrive in LA, in order to adjust faster to the time zone. It's a good excuse to head straight out and explore your local restaurants!

6. Due to the 8-hour time difference between the UK and LA, it's likely that you'll wake up between 3-5am on your first morning feeling hungry. Prepare for this and have a snack available should you need it.

TRAVEL INSURANCE

7. Medical care is expensive in the US and there's no equivalent to the UK's free National Health Service. Purchase travel insurance if visiting under an ESTA, or look into Medical Insurance if relocating on a Visa.

8. When comparing different insurance policies, check the maximum length of stay is a similar length to the maximum on your ESTA or Visa to ensure the policy would be valid.

9. If moving across to LA with work, ensure your employer covers you with business travel insurance. Also arrange your own personal travel insurance so you're covered during the week, at the weekends, and on days off work.

MAKING A HOME

WHERE TO LIVE

10. Explore neighbourhoods close to where you work. Rush-hour traffic is notoriously bad in LA and a shorter commute will improve your daily life.

11. Popular rental websites for house hunting include Hotpads, Padmapper, The Rental Girl, West Side Rentals, and Zillow.

12. Read reviews about the landlord/apartment complex on Yelp, especially if you're unsure about a place.

13. Before you sign a lease, stay in a nearby Airbnb for a few days to get a feel for the area and test the commute.

14. Under California law, Renters Insurance isn't legally required; however, landlords may require it as a term of leasing.

15. Under California law, the total security deposit for an unfurnished apartment must not exceed 2 months' rent. For a furnished apartment the cap is 3 months' rent.

BUYING HOMEWARE

16. Properties are usually let unfurnished and not all landlords supply fridges or stoves - don't be alarmed if you have to buy your own!

17. You can buy household items and furniture in stores such as AllModern, HomeDepot, HomeGoods, IKEA and Target.

18. Discover home furnishings and decor bargains on second-hand websites such as OfferUp and Craigslist, or in Goodwill stores.

19. Americans use a sheet, a 'comforter' (duvet) and a quilt, instead of a duvet in a duvet cover. If you're searching the aisles for duvet covers you'll be there a very long time!

20. Buy a small toolkit to help you easily assemble and hang items. Your life will be much easier and you can sell it on OfferUp once you're finished.

21. Los Angeles is very near the San Andreas Fault. Ensure you've packed an earthquake survival kit bag and have it easily accessible, it could save your life.

UTILITIES

22. The most popular Internet and TV providers are:
    - AT&T
    - DirecTV
    - DISH
    - Frontier
    - HughesNet
    - Spectrum
    - Verizon

23. The main Electricity, Gas and Water providers are:
    - Los Angeles Department of Water and Power
    - Southern California Edison
    - Southern California Gas Company

24. Electricity voltages differ to the UK, so leave behind items such as hairdryers and straighteners which will not work properly and buy them out in the US.

25. Remember to bring UK to US plug adaptors with you for smaller items such as phone and laptop chargers.

GETTING AROUND

PUBLIC TRANSPORT

Los Angeles has extensive public transport systems, allowing visitors and those without cars to have travel independence across the city.

26. The Metro Rail system covers a large area along six lines. Purchase a reusable TAP card at the station to ride. Base fares start at $1.75.

27. Metro Bus has more than 200 different routes across the greater Los Angeles area. It services the Metro Rail stations as well as surrounding National Parks. You can pay in cash or using the TAP card, and fares start at $1.75.

28. The LADOT Commuter Express offers a fast bus service to Downtown LA. Fares vary by pass type.

29. Uber and Lyft carpools are cheaper than in the UK. Beware of prolonged journey times during rush hour (5-10am and 3-7pm).

30. The Amtrak rail system travels to major cities across the US. It departs LA from the iconic Union Station.

31. Metro Bike Share allows you to hire bikes from docks for $1.75/30 minutes or $5/day. However, unlike the UK, many roads are not bike friendly so ride at your peril! Safer places to ride include the bike lanes in Downtown

LA and The Strand along the Beach Cities, which is separated from cars and has stunning views.

32. Dockless options, such as electric scooters and bikes, are booming in Downtown LA and the Beach Cities. They're easy to use, travel at speed and the best part is you can leave them almost wherever you want (as long as it's out of a no-drop zone and not blocking the path). To ride download the app - such as Bird, Lime, Jump, Uber and Lyft - and upload your driving license. The electric scooters must be ridden on the road, not the pavement, so you need to have a valid driving licence. The cost is around $1 to unlock the scooters and $0.15/minute to ride.

33. It is uncommon to walk far in LA, and if you do, you may find the 'sidewalk' (pavement) stops without warning or option to cross. 'Jaywalking' (crossing roads at points which are not designated crossings) is illegal in parts of California and other states in the US, so it is wise to return to the nearest crossing. You can only walk when the hand flashes white and cars must give you right of way.

34. Do not walk on the streets after dark, especially if you're alone, as it can be unsafe. You may walk around London at night, but this isn't London.

DRIVING

35. If you're thinking about leasing a car, begin by hiring one for the first few weeks whilst you settle in. Get discounted rates through your airline. Most hire cars are automatic.

36. Always carry your driving license with you when driving a vehicle, be it a car or an electric scooter. Failure to do so is against state law and you could be issued with a $250 fine.

37. Drive on the right-hand side of the road.

38. Keep an eye on car indicators, which can flash red instead of orange (if used at all).

39. Vehicles with 2 or more occupants can drive in the HOV (High Occupancy Vehicle) lane, which has a diamond sign. These carpool lanes are often separated by double yellow lines and the entrances/exits can be a few miles apart.

40. You don't need to change lanes to overtake a car; you're allowed to undertake them.

41. You must come to a complete standstill at all stop signs.

42. If traffic lights are flashing red, this indicates a four-way crossing system is temporarily in place. At four-way

crossings the car who stopped first goes first, and it then continues in stopping order.

43. You can turn right at a junction whilst the traffic light is red, unless there's a sign saying otherwise.

44. Beware of pedestrians when turning at junctions. The white hand indicates when they can cross and pedestrians have priority over cars.

45. Expect a slower journey on rainy days and avoid the outside lanes as these can become flooded.

46. Blend in with locals by adding 'the' before the road numbers, e.g. 'the four-oh-five (405)', 'the one-ten (110)'.

47. Locations are spoken as the road name intersections, such as 'Rosecrans and Sepulveda'. You can even type this into Google Maps.

48. To pay for 'gas' (petrol) at the pump, you need to enter a numerical zip-code. Therefore, if your bank card is registered to a UK address you cannot do this and will have to pre-pay the attendant inside, before filling up.

49. Want to know the secret to hands-free filling at the gas pump? There's a small metal flap inside the nozzle handle. It's a game changer. Now you can just stand there...or clean the flies off your windows with the supplied sponges next to every pump!

50. If you see an emergency vehicle approaching you using its siren and/or flashing red lights, you must pull to the right side of the road and stop until the emergency vehicle has passed.

51. If you're pulled over by the Police do NOT get out of your car, as this is seen as a threat. Instead, put your hands on the steering wheel or dashboard where they can be seen. If it's night time, quickly turn on the inside light before placing your hands on the dashboard. Answer questions succinctly and do not make jokes.

52. Driving laws differ by state, read up on the local rules before you drive anywhere new.

PARKING RULES

53. Park in the same direction as traffic. If you park facing oncoming vehicles you risk a 'ticket' (parking fine).

54. Painted curbs have different meanings:
    Blue – disabled permit holders only
    Green – park for a limited time
    Red – no stopping or parking at any time
    White – pick up or drop off zone
    Yellow – loading area

55. Turn your wheels into the curb when parking on hills. This prevents the car rolling into the road if the brakes fail. If you forget to do this, you may get a ticket.

56. LA parking signs are notoriously lengthy. Read all of the sign to ensure you're not parking on street sweeping day, in a permit-only zone, or during restricted hours.

57. If you are required to pay for an on-street parking space, the meters are directly next to the space. These usually cost $2 an hour and accept card payments. The meters flash green if there's time on the clock or red if it's expired.

58. For Valet parking you're expected to tip at least $3 to $5 when collecting your car, regardless of the service fee.

EVERYDAY LIFE

MONEY & BANKS

59. You will be unable to open an American bank account without a social security number, which you can only get through certain visas or US citizenship.

60. UK banks may charge transaction and withdrawal fees if you use your UK banks cards in the US, so check what these are before you start buying items.

61. Pre-paid currency cards such as Caxton and Monzo are free from transaction and withdrawal charges. Read the small print to check if they charge interest or have additional charges after set spend limits.

62. ATMs charge fees to withdraw cash, which start at $3. 'Drive-thru' ATMs exist!

63. Items may cost more at the till than advertised on the shelf. This is because price tags exclude 'sales tax' (VAT), which differs by state.

64. The expected tip is 15-20% for any service-related payment, for example in a restaurant, a bar, a taxi, or at the hairdressers. If you tip less than 10% they'll ask you what's wrong with the service!

PHONES

65. Most people buy 'cell phones' (mobiles) through AT&T or Verizon. Both companies require large, upfront payments in the absence of credit history. If moving with work, go through your employer to secure a cheaper deal.

66. If you're only staying in LA for a few months, consider using your UK phone with a Google Fi plan. You will receive a US number and billing is simple as the rates apply worldwide.

67. Save money when you chat with family and friends in the UK by using WhatsApp, which uses your phone's internet connection instead of your data allowance.

FOOD & SUPERMARKETS

68. Supermarkets are 'grocery stores', trolleys are 'carts', and tills are 'registers'.

69. Popular grocery stores include Gelson's, Pavilions, Ralphs, Trader Joe's and Vons.

70. Popular health food stores include Erewhon, Lassens, Rainbow Acres and WholeFoods.

71. Milk types are: 1%, 2%, Whole and Half & Half. The latter is a mix of milk and cream and is intended for coffee. Most milk is fortified with vitamins and minerals.

72. Eggs are found in the refrigerated section and you must store them in the fridge, due to the increased risk of salmonella contamination.

73. Grated cheese is labelled as 'Shredded Cheese', and a mature cheddar is called 'Sharp Cheddar'.

74. When buying alcohol:

   • You must be 21 or older.

   • You have to pay at a manned register, as opposed to the self-scan registers, as you will be 'carded' (ID'd) by a person.

• UK Driving Licenses are usually accepted as a valid form of ID, although some stores may ask for your passport.

• All members of your group need to present valid ID.

75. Save money by signing up to grocery store loyalty cards, which reduce item prices instantly at the register instead of using a points system.

76. Your items will be bagged up for you at the checkout and you're not expected to tip for this service. Enjoy standing there like a lemon!

77. You can buy cereal, tins of fruit and other packaged food in pharmacies such as CVS and Walgreens.

78. The oven setting 'Broil' is for grilling food and 'Bake' is for roasting.

79. It's acceptable to ask for a box at the end of a restaurant meal and take leftovers home.

WORKING ENVIRONMENT

80. You will be given hugs as greetings. If it's going to feel awkward, jump in first with a British handshake.

81. Work ethic revolves around the American dream - anyone can be successful if you're determined and willing to work hard enough.

82. The absence of friendly greetings, niceties or sign-offs in emails from 'co-workers' (colleagues) may come across as direct and rude, but it's nothing personal and is a common way of working within the US.

83. The US date format is month/date/year. Save yourself confusion by writing the month in letters, for example Mar-9 instead of 3/9.

84. For free conference calls, both within the US and back to the UK, use Zoom.

85. Want to spread happiness? Bring in a box of Randy's Donuts, or a dog.

VISITING A DOCTOR

86. If moving with work, talk to your employer to understand what your options are if you need medical assistance whilst in LA.

87. For medical emergencies call 9-1-1. Fire engines react faster than ambulances, so one will be sent out to assess you first. If the first responders deem you need to go to hospital in an ambulance, they will arrange it but you will be charged an ambulance transport fee, which starts at $600.

88. It can be expensive to visit a hospital or call out a doctor. For non-emergency assistance, locate your nearest Urgent Care centre and check the prices there.

89. Pharmacies, such as CVS and Walgreens, also offer walk-in services. You will be charged for a 30-minute session and there is a price list on their websites. The CVS website allows you to join the queue virtually and then check-in when you arrive in person, so that you can hold your place in the 'line' (queue).

WEATHER

90. Los Angeles is known for its sunshine, averaging 284 sunny days per year.

91. The rainy season is from October to April. When it rains it pours!

92. Temperatures increase with distance from the coast, so inland LA is several degrees warmer and less windy than by the ocean. The hottest month is August and the coldest month is January.

93. Learn the following Fahrenheit banding:

°F	°C	Description
50s	10 - 15	Cold. Wear a jacket.
60s	15 - 21	Mild. Bring a jacket.
70s	21 - 27	Warm. You will be grateful for air-con.
80s	27 - 32	Hot. You understand the obsession with ice-cold drinks.
90s	32 - 37	Really hot. Shade becomes a key commodity.
+100	+37	Really, really hot. You marvel at how cacti survive in the desert.

94. Whilst winter mornings and evenings are cold, you can still burn at midday in winter as the sun is strong all year round.

95. The 'Marine Layer', 'May Gray' and 'June Gloom' refer to a thick band of cloud, prevalent in early-summer mornings along the coast. It is caused by a temperature inversion, where hot air from inland sits above denser air cooled by the ocean. Typically, these overcast skies burn off around lunch time to reveal bright blue skies.

96. If you've watched the film *The Holiday* you'll have heard of the Santa Ana winds. These are strong, dry winds from the deserts inland, and are most common from October to March. They are associated with wildfires as their dryness increases the risk of fires spreading.

OTHER

97. The United States Postal Services (USPS) have blue on-street 'mail' (post) boxes and many store locations. You can also send items through courier companies, such as FedEx and UPS.

98. Measurements are in US Customary Units:

Conversion Table

Type	US	UK
Distance	1 Inch 1 Foot 1 Mile	2.54 Centimeters 0.30 Meters 1.61 Kilometers
Weight	1 Ounce 1 Pound	28.35 Grams 0.45 Kilograms
Volume	1 US Pint 1 US Gallon	0.83 Imperial Pint 3.79 Liters

99. Clothing sizes:

Women's

US	International	UK
2	XS	6
4	XS	8
6	S	10
8	S	12
10	M	14
12	M	16
14	L	18
16	L	20

Men's

US	International	UK
30	XS	30
32	XS	32
34	S	34
36	S	36
38	M	38
40	M	40
42	L	42
44	L	44

100. Shoe sizes:

Women's

US	UK	Europe
4	2	35
5	3	36
6	4	37
7	5	38
8	6	39
9	7	40
10	8	41
11	9	42
12	10	43

Men's

US	UK	Europe
6	5	40
7	6	41
8	7	42
9	8	43
10	9	44
11	10	45
12	11	46
13	12	47
14	13	48
15	14	49

101. Common translations:

English (USA)	English (UK)
Apartment	Flat
Arugula	Rocket (salad)
Blinker	Indicator
Calendar	Diary
Carded	ID'd
Cell Phone	Mobile Phone
Check	Cheque
Chips	Crisps
Cilantro	Coriander
Cookie	Biscuit
Counterclockwise	Anti-clockwise
Co-worker	Colleague
Crosswalk	Crossing
Diary	Journal
Eggplant	Aubergine
Elevator	Lift
Eraser	Rubber
Fall	Autumn
First Floor	Ground Floor
Fries	Chips
Hood	Bonnet
Line	Queue
Mail	Post

Main Street	High Street
Overalls	Dungarees
Period	Full Stop
Register	Till
Restroom	Toilet
Rubber	Condom
Second Floor	First Floor
Sidewalk	Pavement
Sneakers	Trainers
Sweater	Jumper
Takeout	Takeaway
Third Floor	Second Floor
Ticket	Fine (£££)
Traffic Circle	Roundabout
Trash	Rubbish
Trash Can	Bin
Truck	Lorry
Trunk	Boot
Turn-out	Lay-by
Vacation	Holiday
Windshield	Windscreen
Zip Code	Post Code
Zucchini	Courgette

A NOTE FROM THE AUTHOR

Thank you so much for buying this guide, I hope you found it useful and that you love living in LA as much as I did.

If you enjoyed reading this, I would greatly appreciate a short review on Amazon, especially if you write it whilst waiting for your car to fill up with petrol or the check-out person to fill your shopping bags. That would be very efficient, and less awkward than standing like a lemon. Reviews are crucial and even just a line or two can make a huge difference.

Many thanks and in true LA style; I appreciate you!

Charlotte

WEBSITES

ARRIVING

- ESTA application - esta.cbp.dhs.gov/esta
- Global Entry - cbp.gov/travel/trusted-traveler-programs/global-entry
- US Embassy - Visas - uk.usembassy.gov/visas

MAKING A HOME

- Airbnb - airbnb.com
- AllModern - allmodern.com
- Craigslist - losangeles.craigslist.org
- Earthquake Survival Kit - cdc.gov/disasters/earthquakes/supplies.html
- Goodwill - goodwill.org
- HomeDepot - homedepot.com
- HomeGoods - homegoods.com
- Hotpads - hotpads.com
- IKEA - ikea.com
- OfferUp - offerup.com (note - website only works from the US)
- Padmapper - padmapper.com
- Target - target.com
- TheRentalGirl - therentalgirl.com
- Trulia - trulia.com
- West Side Rentals - westsiderentals.com

- Yelp - yelp.com
- Zillow - zillow.com

GETTING AROUND

- Amtrak - amtrak.com
- AT&T - att.com
- Bird - bird.co
- DirecTV - directv.com
- DISH - dish.com
- Frontier - frontier.com
- HughesNet - hughesnet.com
- Jump - jump.com
- LADOT Commuter Express - ladottransit.com
- Lime - li.me
- Local driving rules - drivinglaws.aaa.com
- Los Angeles Department of Water and Power - ladwp.com
- Lyft - lyft.com
- Metro Bike Share - bikeshare.metro.net
- Metro Bus and Rail - metro.net
- Southern California Edison - sce.com
- Southern California Gas Company - socalgas.com
- Spectrum - spectrum.com
- Uber - uber.com
- Verizon - verizonwireless.com

EVERYDAY LIFE

- Caxton - caxtonfx.com
- CVS - cvs.com
- Erewhon - erewhonmarket.com
- FedEx - fedex.com
- Gelson's - gelsons.com
- Google Fi - fi.google.com
- Lassens - lassens.com
- Monzo - monzo.com
- Pavilions - pavilions.com
- Rainbow Acres - rainbowacresca.com
- Ralphs - ralphs.com
- Randy's Donuts - randysdonuts.com
- Trader Joe's - traderjoes.com
- United States Postal Services - usps.com
- UPS - ups.com
- Vons - vons.com
- Walgreens - walgreens.com
- WhatsApp - whatsapp.com
- WholeFoods - wholefoodsmarket.com
- Zoom - zoom.us

ABOUT THE AUTHOR

Charlotte Harris moved from London to Los Angeles to help set up a coconut yogurt brand. During her year in LA, she fell in love with exploring the palm tree lined streets, snow-capped mountains, and sandy beaches. She was inspired to write this guide after walking into a bank thinking it was a supermarket.

Printed in Great Britain
by Amazon

70625646R00031